Everyone Loves King Julien!

Maurice

Xixi

King Julien

Adapted by Benjamin Hulme-Cross

King Julien was watching television with Maurice.

"Here is the news," said Xixi. "We asked people if they liked King Julien, and nearly everyone said yes!"

"What? That means some of my people do *not* like me!" cried King Julien.

"*Most* people like you!" said Maurice.

"This is terrible!" cried King Julien.

King Julien sent Maurice to find out how many people didn't like him.

"Who likes King Julien?" asked Maurice.

Nearly everyone said they did, but some people looked grumpy.

"Perhaps they don't like King Julien," Maurice said to himself.

"How can I make *all* my people like me?"
wondered King Julien.

"I know! I'll give them mangoes! Everybody will love me, because everyone loves mangoes!" he said.

So he took a large box of mangoes up into a tree and threw them down to everyone.

"Catch!" cried King Julien.

"Free mangoes! We love King Julien!" they cried.
The lemurs stretched out and grabbed the mangoes.

Suddenly, there were no mangoes left.
They had run out!

"Maybe they don't want any more?"
said King Julien.

"More mangoes!" they all cried, and they jumped onto the branch.

"Stop! You are all too heavy for the tree!" cried King Julien.

The branch was breaking off, and there was a little lemur baby right under the tree!

Creak!

Groan!

"Oh no!" cried King Julien.

King Julien jumped down, ran
to the baby and snatched him up.
Then he ran as fast as he could.

Wallop! Smash!

The huge branch fell with a crash, but the baby was safe!

So now *everyone* loved King Julien!